CONTENTS

Preface ii
Ollie Acorn Seed (Front Cover Puzzle) 1

Activities with Trees

"Tree Talk" with Ollie Acorn 2
Acorn Adventures 3
Seeds and Leaves 5
See-a-Seed Shape 7
Travel'n Seed Experiment 8
Bounce, Float and Spin 11
Leaf and Seed Mobile 13
Build-a-Tree 15

Activities with Animals

Animal Aids 17
Furry Farmers and Hitchhiker Seeds 19
Sticky Seed Experiment 20
Science Sing-a-Long 21
Biology Bingo 23
Mother Nature's Co-op Kitchen 26

Oliver Oak Tree (Back Cover Puzzle) 27
Teacher/Parent Guide 28

PREFACE

Young children possess a healthy curiosity about the natural world around them. This book was designed not only to present interesting facts about living things but also to involve the young child in meaningful activities that will promote understanding, sharpen observational skills, and initiate scientific problem solving with simple experimentation.

The first section of the book focuses on trees, nature's largest and most impressive plants, and investigates types common to all states and climes, for example, oak, maple and poplar. A tiny seed mascot, known as Ollie Acorn, introduces the children to various characteristics of these leafy giants with picture fill-ins, songs, games and experimental projects.

This is followed by a related section on animals, establishing their interdependence with the Plant Kingdom. Again, indoor and outdoor experimentation, songs and games make this an exciting learning experience. Ollie Acorn continues to be the children's nature guide, pictured as a young sapling and, finally, in the role of Oliver Oak Tree.

The experiments outlined throughout the text can successfully be accomplished in the fall, with easily located seed specimens. Most are also possible in winter and spring, utilizing the alternative suggestion.

We hope that through these activities, familiar seasonal occurrences will take on new interest and meaning as your **Young Scientists Explore the World of Nature.**

Sincerely,

Linda Penn

"Tree Talk" with Ollie Acorn

Trees are nature's giant plants. Trees grOW _____, _____, and _____. A special _____ named Ollie Acorn grew up in a White Oak _____. White Oaks are not white in color. The white is just a name. Their cousin is the Red Oak _____ whose _____ and _____ are not the same.

| White Oak Leaf and Acorn Seed | | Red Oak Leaf and Acorn Seed |

| leaves | seeds | tree | flowers |

Seeds and Leaves

I'll stay hidden away in the ground until spring

when Poplar and Maple grow seeds that have wings.

While Poplar seeds parachute

Maple will flutter.

Connect the seed and its leaf.
Don't mix one with the other!

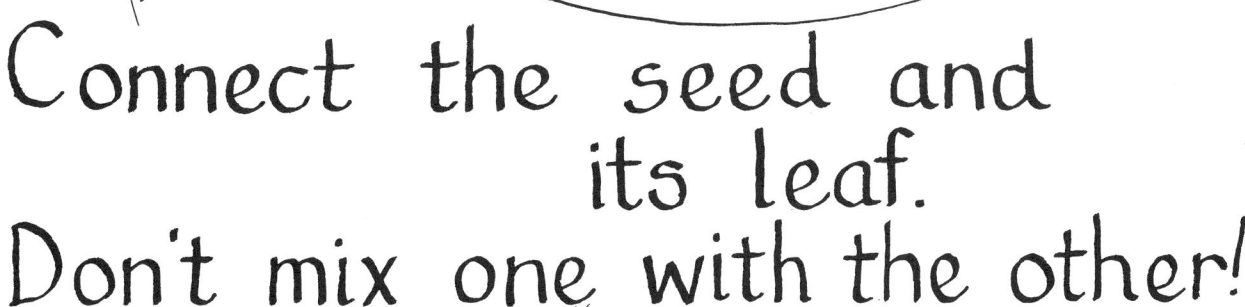

Wrong   Right

See-a-Seed Shape

Acorns can bounce with their circular shapes.

Poplar seeds float and triangles make.

Maple seed ovals are often seen twirling.

Try and trace the seed shapes,

set your pencil a-whirling!

Tree Seed Tally	
⬭ ovals	
◯ circles	
▽ triangles	

Travel'n Seed Experiment

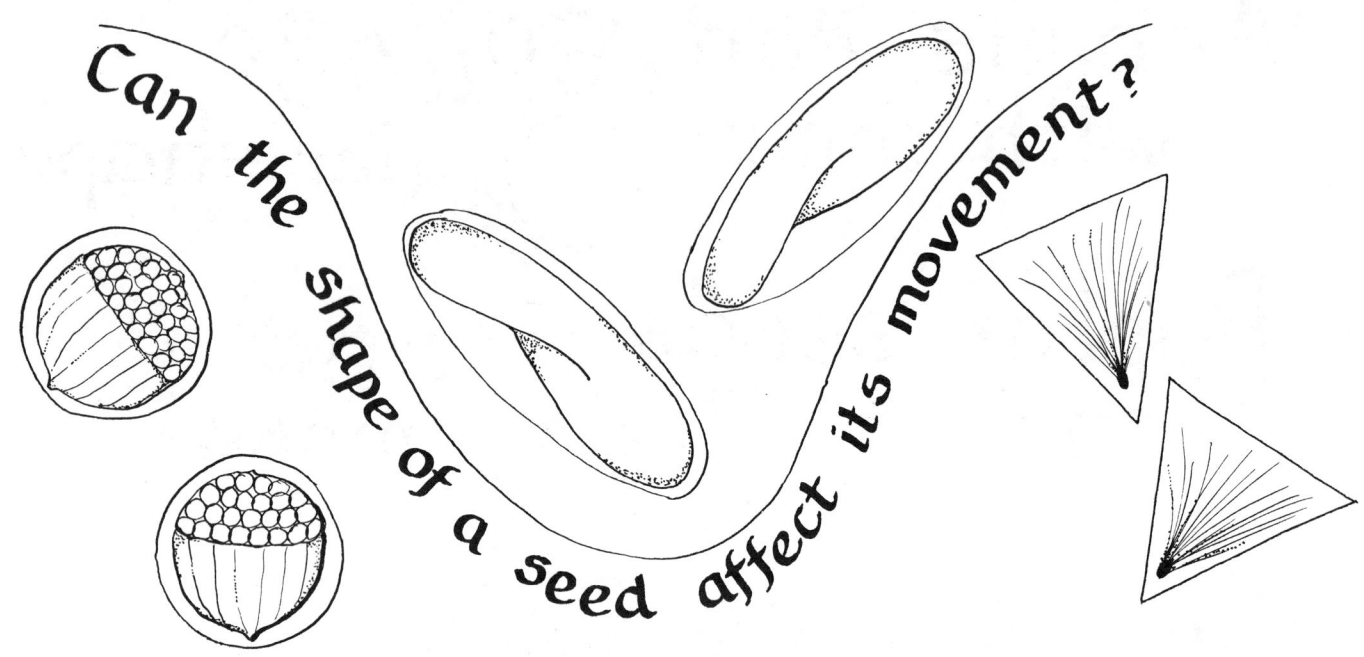

Can the shape of a seed affect its movement?

Materials needed:

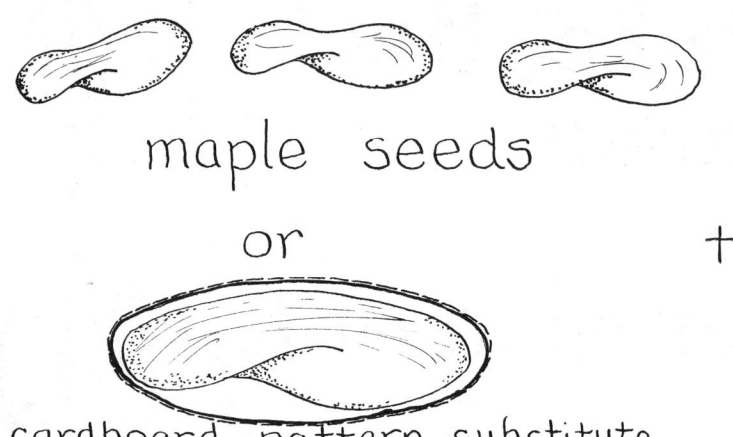

maple seeds

or

cardboard pattern substitute

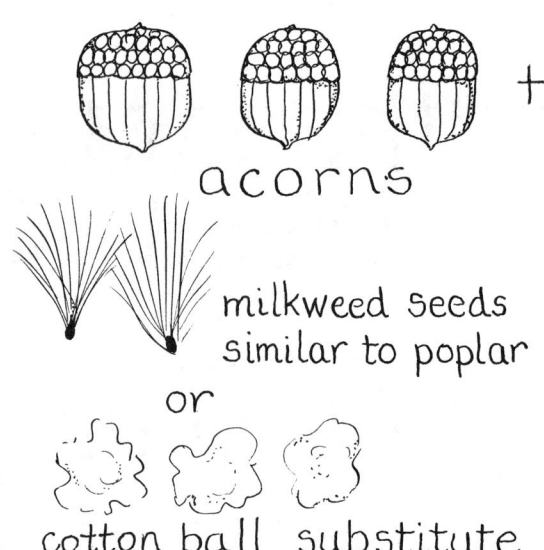

acorns

+

milkweed seeds similar to poplar

or

cotton ball substitute

Discussion:
1. Observe actual seeds and relate to shapes pictured above.
   Place a seed of each type on similar shapes shown on the next page.

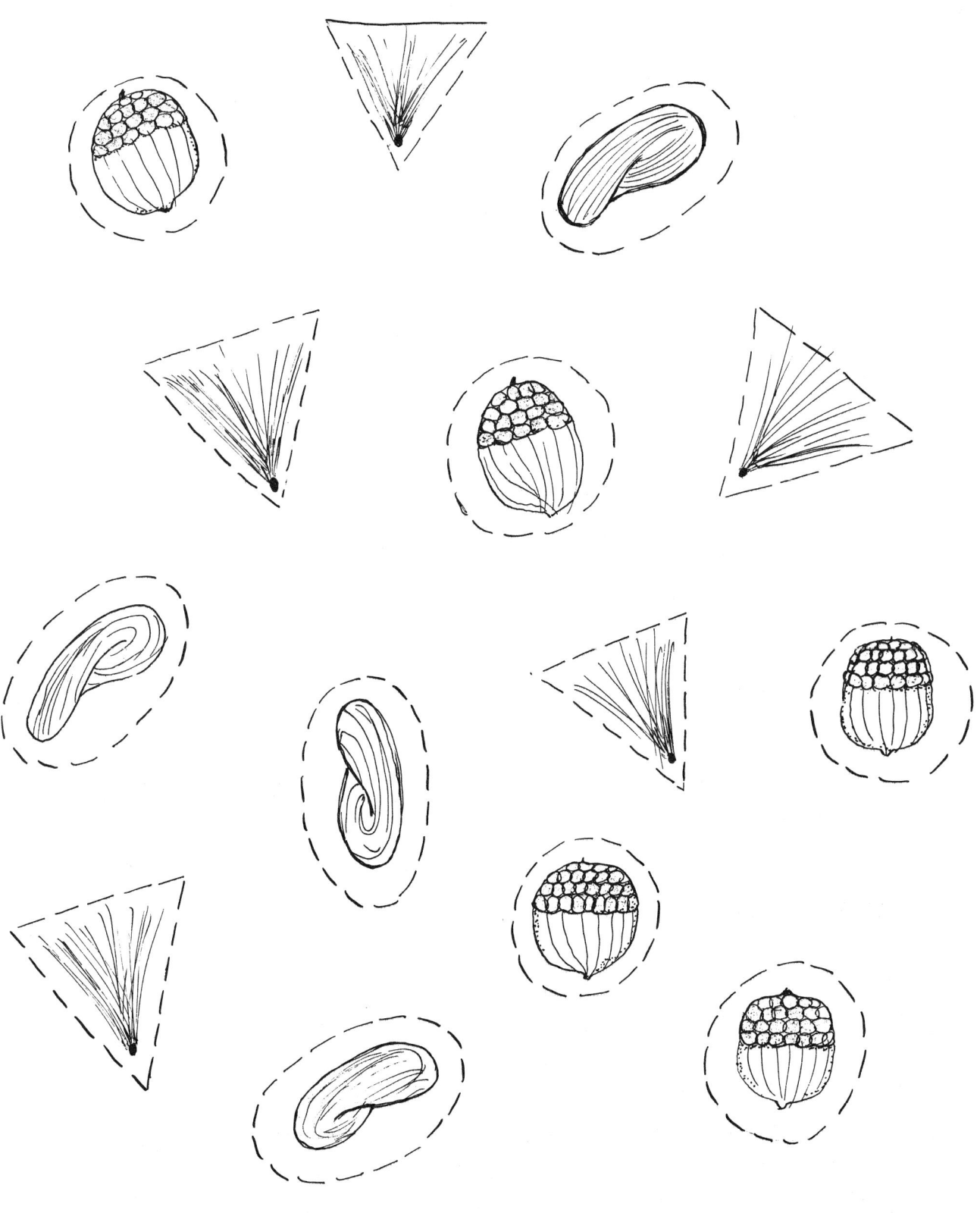

Rolling on...

2. Discuss the motion of a circular ball.

rolling and bouncing

3. Discuss the motion of a triangular kite.

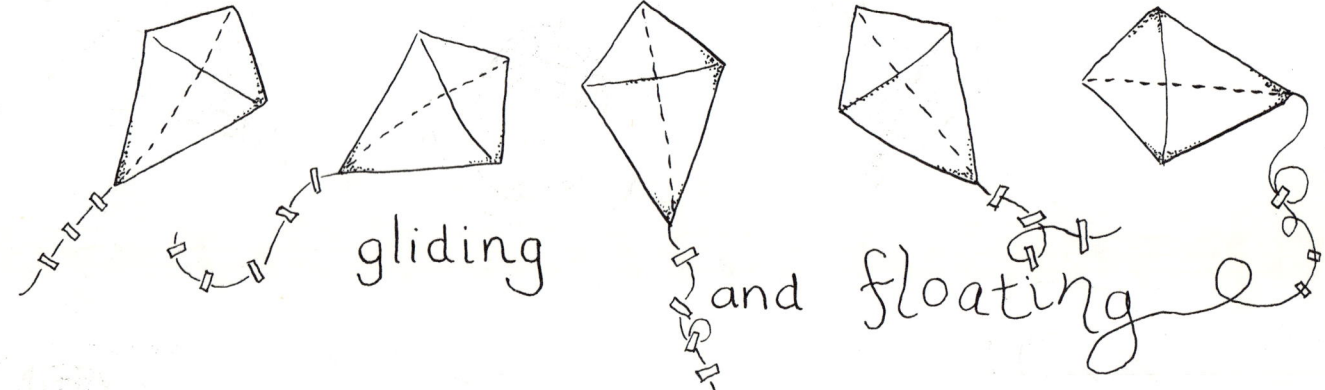

gliding and floating

4. Discuss oval-shaped airplane propellers.

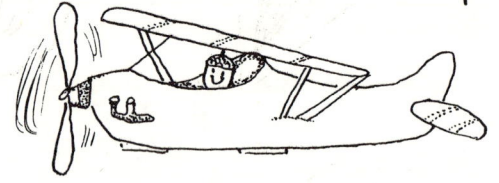

spinning

Experiment:

1. Drop a seed from a high point in the room. Observe motion in the air for 🥜 and 🌱. Upon reaching the floor, for 🌰.
2. Have children imitate observed motion.
3. If cotton ball substitute is used, child pulls off a small piece and blows it from a high point.

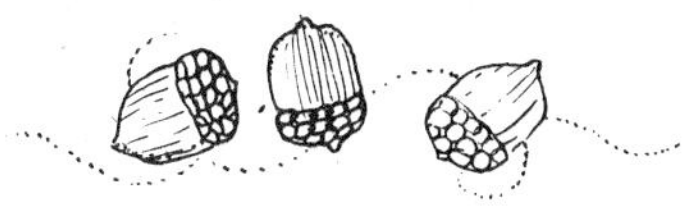

HOW TO PLAY GAME

TRAVEL'N SEED

1. Select three "tree leaders" to wear poplar, oak or maple leaves. Stand leaders apart at one end of room.
2. Fill "Seed Sack" with seed pictures cut from master. Shake sack to scramble.
3. Children pick seeds and bounce (acorn), float (poplar), or spin (maple) to proper "tree leader." If movement is incorrect, turn is lost.
4. The "tree" with the most "seeds" wins.

Variation: Real acorns and maple seeds may be substituted for pictures, and cotton balls for poplar seed pictures.

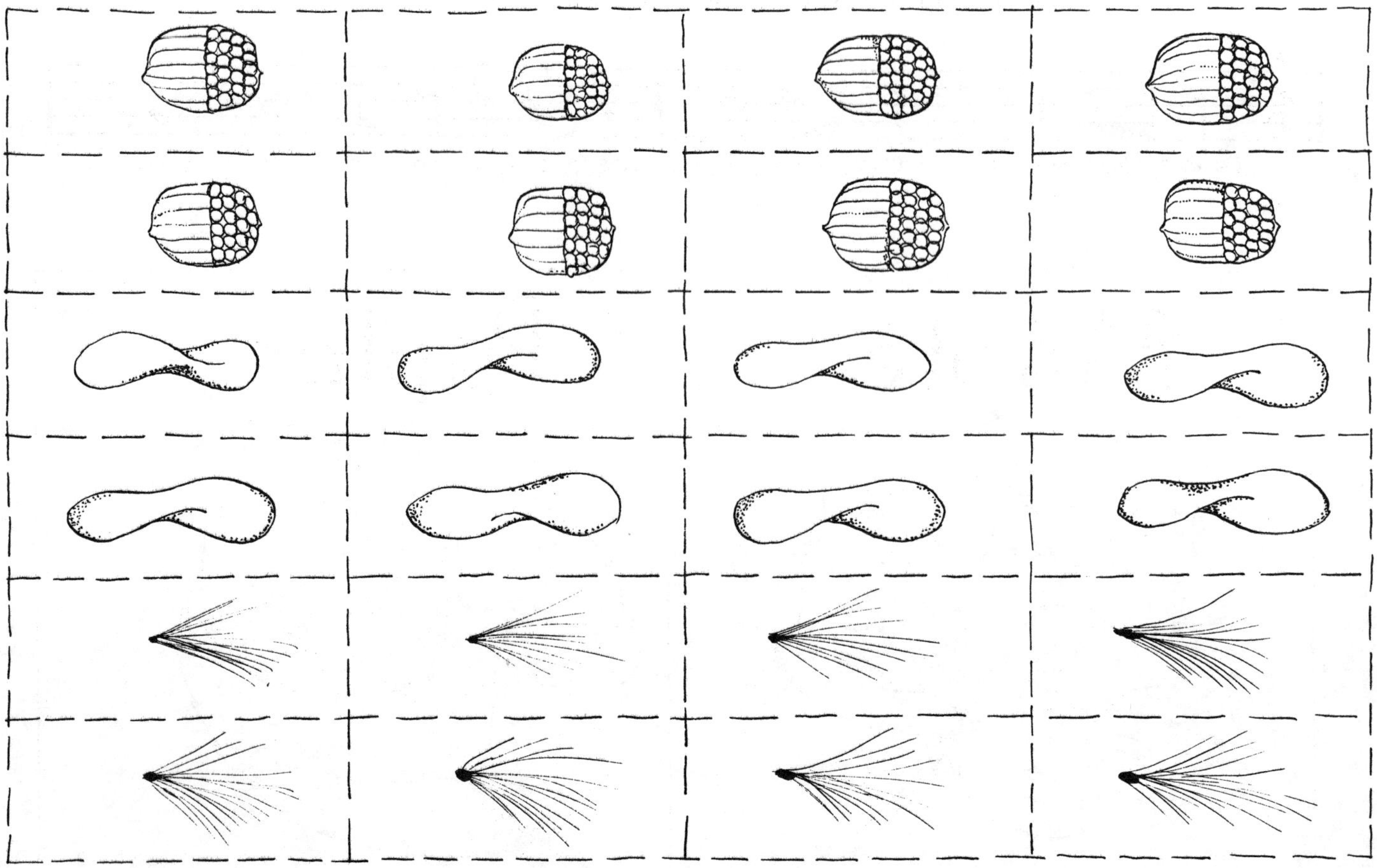

Leaf & Seed Mobile

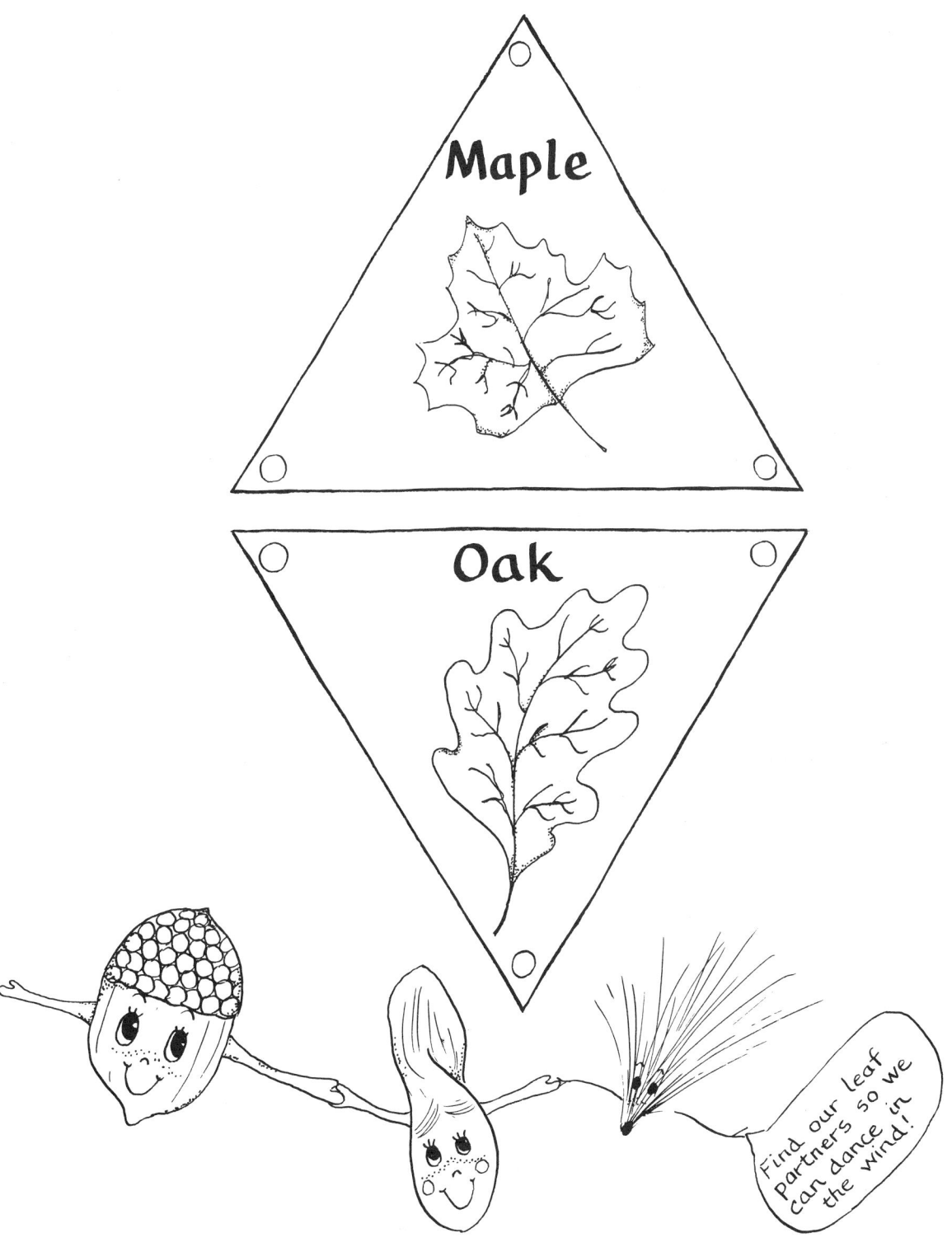

Find our leaf partners so we can dance in the wind!

Mount on tagboard

Leaf & Seed Mobile

Poplar

14

Build·a·Tree

If I'm planted in the ground just right,

with plenty of rain and bright sunlight,

you know what I'll grow up to be?

A tall and mighty White Oak Tree....

Acorn-seed

Bark

Trunk

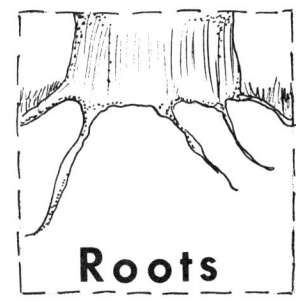
Roots

Branches

Leaves

Flower-Catkin

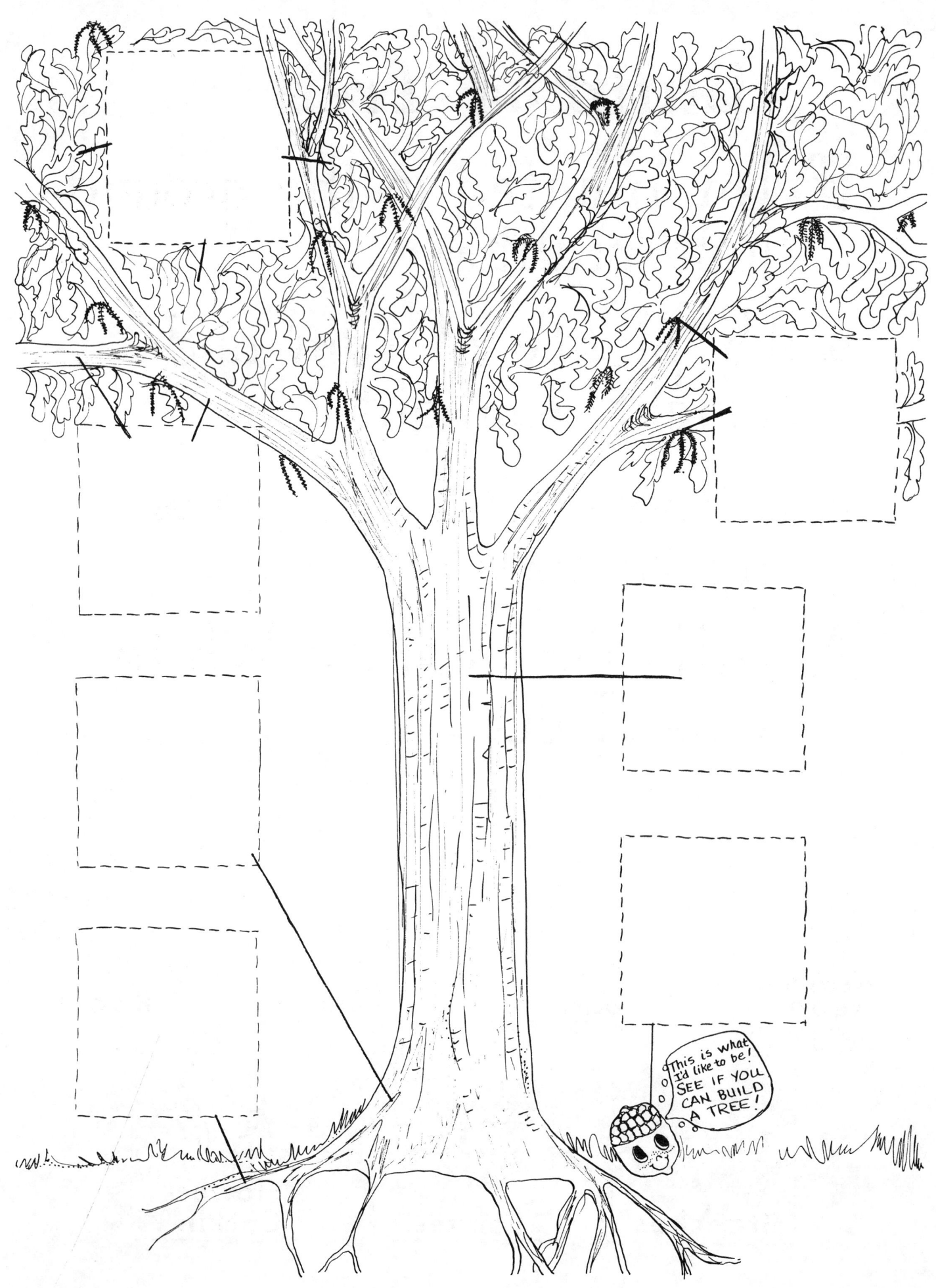

Animal Aids

If we could talk to the animals,
they wouldn't even know,
that things they do
help plant seeds grOW!

Two kinds of insects pictured
above find flowers are sweet,
for it's nectar they (love)!
Mark the insects in the air
with a [square],

since they spread seed powder (pollen)
with their leg and body hair.
Birds eating seeds and berries
 are not very neat.
They scatter their food
 whenever they eat.
Without these messy eaters
seeds might stay on plants, you know,
 and they would not be able
 to find a spot to grOW!
 (circle the birds in the bush.)
In fall, the squirrels will bury nuts.
Soon they're covered with
 winter's snow.
Should these seeds stay hidden
 until spring,
some tiny trees will start to grow.
(I bury nut seeds in the ground.
 Color me brown.)

Furry Farmers and Hitchhiker Seeds

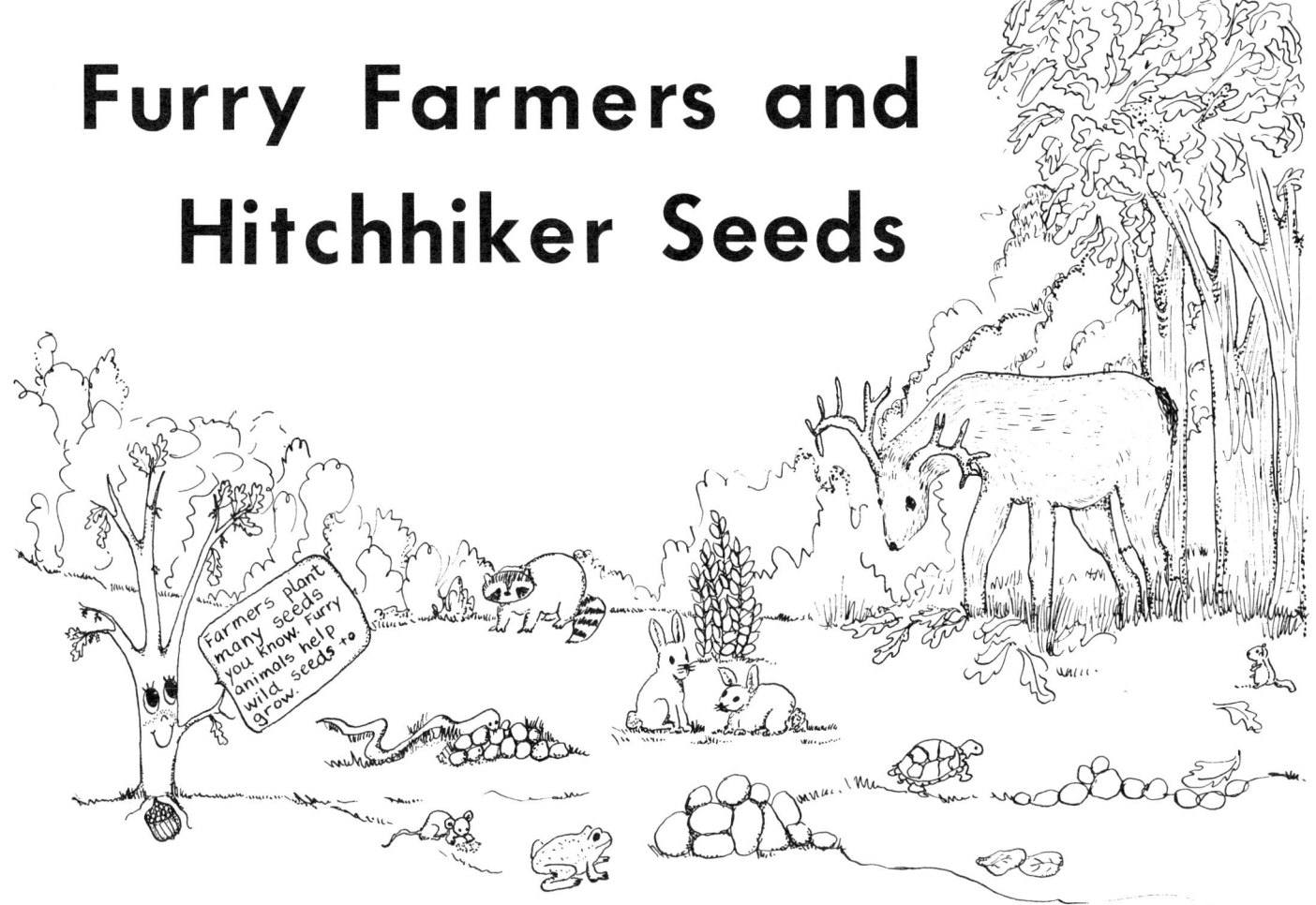

Some seeds can fly
 while others like to stick.
"Stickers" wait for furry animals,
 then hitch a ride quick!
As an animal moves by them,
these seeds catch on their fur
and travel till they drop off
or are picked off like a burr.
 Color the furry animals.

Sticky Seed Experiment

Question: Do "hitchhiker" seeds stick best on "smooth" or "furry" surfaces?

glue wax paper here	glue textured or *fuzzy* material here
Smooth side - like turtle shell or snake skin.	Furry side - like rabbit, chipmunk or racoon.

Step 1   Take a "Weed Walk" in a field in the fall. Wear long pants. Pin a square of textured material to pant cuff.

Step 2   Unpin square. Pick off "hitchhiker" seeds and drop on prepared experiment paper.

Alternatives: 1. Cut textured material into tiny pieces (like the "hitchhiker" seeds). Drop on prepared experiment paper. 2. Have children gather seeds in a field near their homes and bring to school for this experiment. In fall, large quantities of wild carrot seeds are available. They can be found in the dried Queen Anne's lace flower. Be sure to look at carrot seeds with a magnifying glass. A commercially sold package of carrot seeds can be used as a substitute for wild seeds.

Science Sing-a-Long

Some things change form completely
from the time
 that they begin.
When you sing
 the "Meta, Meta" song
just put
 their names in...

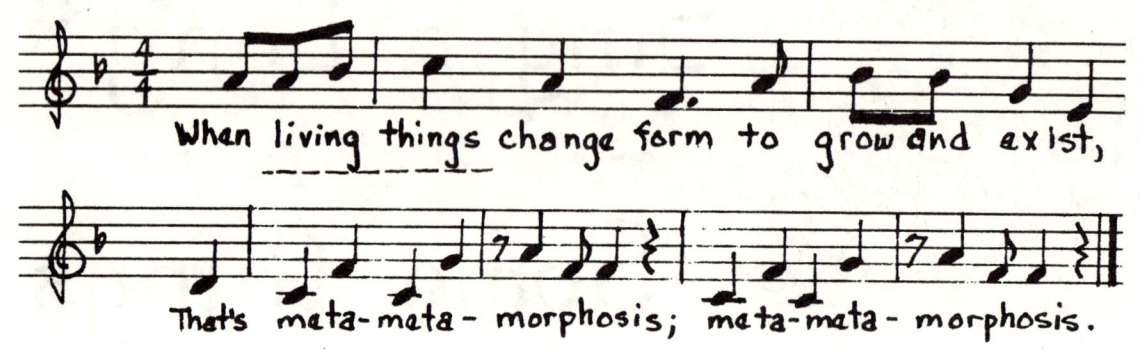

Meta, Meta Morphosis

When living things change form to grow and exist,
That's meta-meta-morphosis; meta-meta-morphosis.

dirty flies

mosquitoes

frogs and toads

butterflies

lightning bugs

ants and bees

ladybugs

Biology Bingo

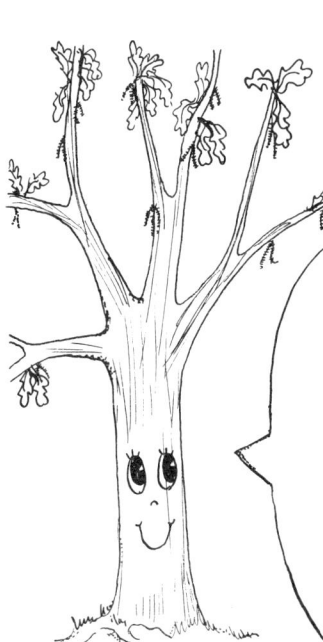

It's fun learning about life, how things change as they grow. Fill in the empty squares and play Biology Bingo!

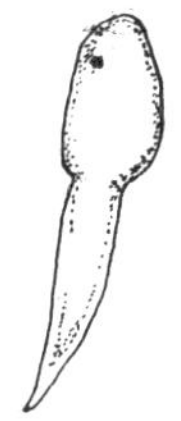

tadpole	 child	 butterfly	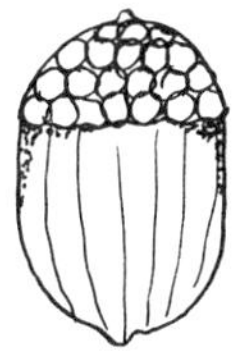 acorn seed
 adult	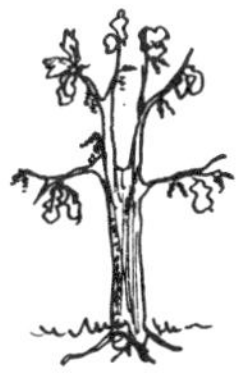 sapling	 eggs of frog	 caterpillar
 butterfly egg	 Oak tree	 teen-ager	 froglet

Cut and paste in appropriate squares in Bingo matrix on facing page.

23

Bio Bingo   *Bio Bingo*

	Stage 1	Stage 2	Stage 3	Stage 4
	baby			
		rooted acorn		
			pupa-chrysalis	
				frog

Rules for playing Biology Bingo can be found on the following page.

Directions for Biology Bingo:

1. Divide children into four teams. Assign each team a species name. (Also, can be played by 2 to 4 players. If 2 players, each is assigned two species.)
   Each child will need 16 markers.

2. Adult acts as caller, using a completed Bingo matrix cut into individual cards. Shuffle cards.

3. First "species" to complete life cycle calls "Bingo." Play continues, to establish 2nd, 3rd. and 4th. places. Repeat game for as long as time allows, shuffling cards before beginning again.

4. Scoring:
   1st place finish scores .... 4 points
   2nd place .... 3 points
   3rd place .... 2 points
   4th place .... 1 point
   Total the points at end of game session to determine the winning team.

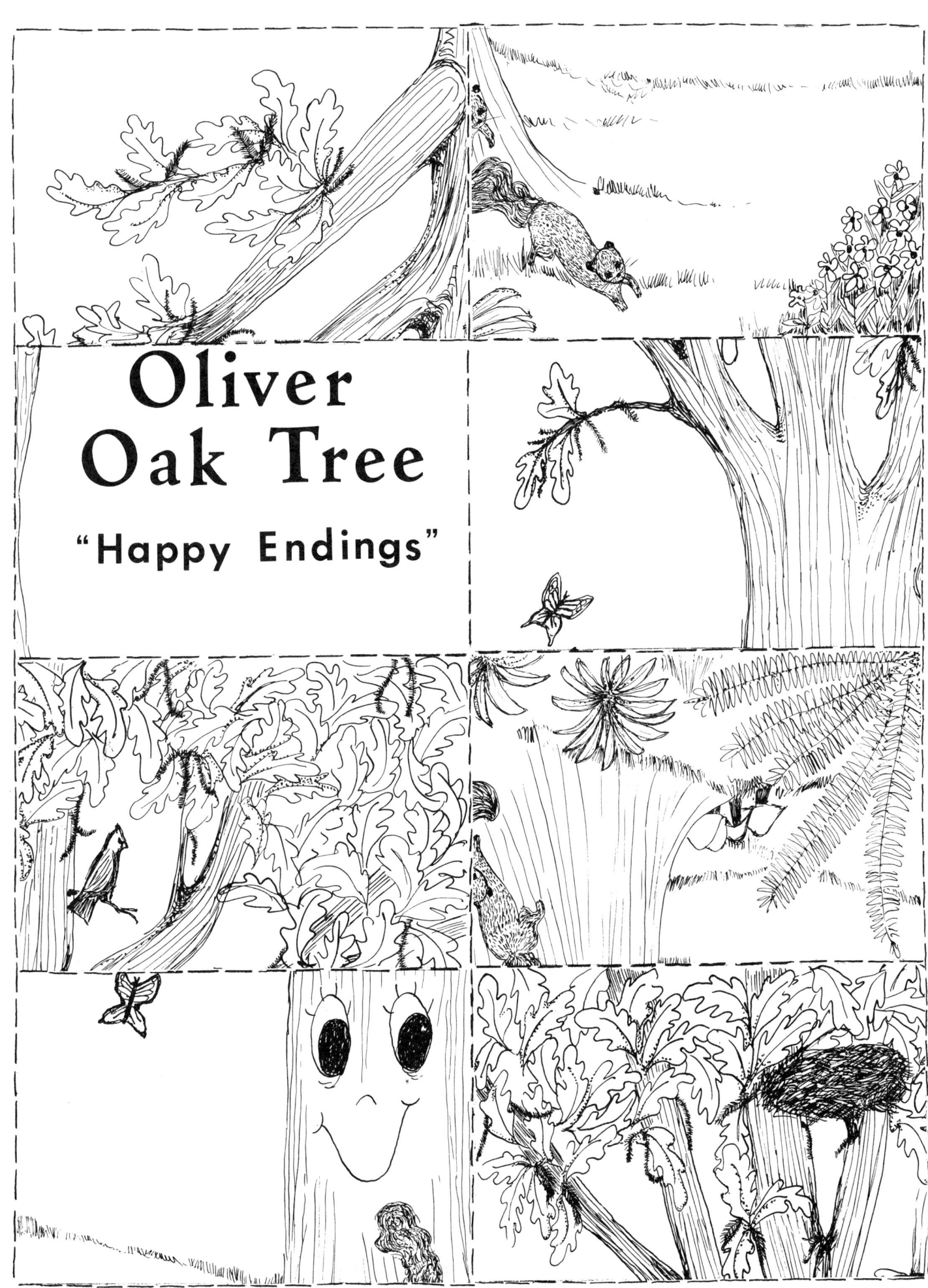

TEACHER/PARENT GUIDE

OLLIE ACORN SEED "A Beginning" (p.1)

DISCUSSION: Have the children watched squirrels burying acorns in the fall? Why are the acorns buried in the ground? (Winter food supply) Do they know squirrels often forget their hiding places? What could happen if a buried acorn seed is forgotten?

LEARNING ACTIVITY: The activity pages begin with a picture puzzle of a squirrel burying a seed, named Ollie Acorn. Little Ollie is not planning on being eaten, but rather that the squirrel will forget his hiding spot, so Ollie can grow into an oak tree. Look for Ollie as a "nature guide" throughout these science activity pages.

Each child can make an Ollie Acorn cover for his/her own nature book, by cutting out the pieces of the puzzle, assembling them, and gluing the completed picture to tagboard. The back cover puzzle, (page 27) may also be completed at this time. By tape-binding the front cover to the back, each child can have a folder to hold the remaining activity sheets as they are completed.

Answer Key: The completed puzzles look like this:

VOCABULARY: acorn, seed, fall, winter

"TREE TALK" with Ollie Acorn (p.2)

DISCUSSION: The differences in trees can be spotted easily by looking at the shapes of their leaves and seeds. Squirrels know there is a difference between the acorn seeds of the white oak (very sweet) and the red oak (bitter). What differences do the children notice in the oak leaves pictured on this page? (rounded edges or pointed edges)... in the acorns? (longer, shorter)

LEARNING ACTIVITY: Take a "Tree Trek" in the fall to look for oak trees. Collect oak leaves and acorn seeds. If you are fortunate to have access to both red and white oaks, have the children compare leaves and acorns from both trees to identify type and qualify as a "Tree Detective." Use the pictures shown on the activity sheet as a guide.

The collected leaves can be pressed with a warm iron, between sheets of wax paper. Peel from paper and have your "detectives" mount on poster board along with the acorns, as "clues" to the oak trees in the area.

Answer Key for missing picture words: flowers, leaves, seeds, seed, tree, tree, leaves, seeds

VOCABULARY: tree, plants, flowers, leaves, white oak, sweet, red oak, bitter.

ACORN ADVENTURES (pp.3-4)

DISCUSSION: The children have noticed acorns, the seeds of oak trees, dropping to the ground in the fall. Many of these acorns are tasty nuts and fall from the trees because they are ripe and ready to be eaten by animals such as squirrels, or stored for winter food. Can the children name some things they like to eat that must be ripe to be tasty? (for example, bananas, apples, peaches, plums, pears)

LEARNING ACTIVITY: To understand the meaning of "ripe," try the Banana Taste Test experiment. Obtain both green and yellow-skinned bananas. Use a napkin or small paper plate divided into sections "1" and "2." (Number sections with a marker.) Place one small slice from each type of banana in a separate section. Have every child determine the "ripe" or "ready-to-eat" banana by tasting. Their conclusions can be charted as shown:

Name	# 1	# 2
Amy		R*
Joe	R	
Sue		R
Lee		R
John		R
*R = Ripe TOTALS:	1	4

Answer Key for Tree Leaf Tally: There are **nine** white oak leaves and **nine** red oak leaves on the ground, across the bottom of pages 3 and 4.

VOCABULARY: ripe, nut

SEEDS AND LEAVES (pp.5-6)

DISCUSSION: The children are now familiar with oak leaves and their acorn seeds. Have they noticed other types of tree leaves and seeds?

LEARNING ACTIVITY: Time for another "Tree Trek" or some "Tree Detective" homework! Have the children locate maple and poplar leaves in the school yard or at home. (Wax leaves as described on page 28 for protected specimens.) Mount each type separately on poster board. After completing the activity on page 6, children can color and cut out seed pictures and labels to add to their leaf display boards.

Answer Key: One-to-one matching--both maple and poplar will have "three" leaf and seed sets. Should match as indicated by pictures on page 5.

VOCABULARY: maple, poplar, spring

SEE-A-SEED SHAPE (p.7)

DISCUSSION: To establish the basic shapes of the three tree seeds pictured, have children name or point out objects in the room that are circular, triangular or oval-shaped.

LEARNING ACTIVITY: Circular acorn seeds are often referred to as tree nuts. Have the children gather a "squirrel salad" of nuts from several different trees. Notice the varying shapes. Sort the nuts first by type, and then find out how many have a basically circular shape like the acorn, for example, walnuts, hickory nuts, hazel nuts. (Tree nuts can also be purchased from grocery stores in the fall and winter months.)

Answer Key:

Tree Seed Tally	
Ovals	4 maple seeds
Circles	5 acorns
Triangles	5 poplar seeds

VOCABULARY: circle, triangle, oval

TRAVEL'N SEED EXPERIMENT (pp.8-10)

DISCUSSION: Discussion ideas presented on pages 8-10.

LEARNING ACTIVITY: Experiment explained on page 10.

A worthwhile addition to the materials needed would be milkweed seeds. These are available in the fall in many areas. The ripened pods, releasing the fluffy topped seeds into the wind, are found in fields and along country roads. They are an excellent substitute for poplar seeds and are best captured with a clear plastic bag. Be careful not to separate the seed from its silky-parachute top. Blow just one of these mildweed seeds into the air and have the children observe its movement. What part does the parachute top play in its movement? How does the slightly heavier seed affect the direction of movement?

VOCABULARY: movement, bouncing, floating, spinning

BOUNCE, FLOAT AND SPIN (pp.11-12)

DISCUSSION: Review the movement observed in the circular acorn, triangular poplar seed and the oval-shaped maple seed. Make sure the children can identify the three types of leaves and their appropriate seeds.

LEARNING ACTIVITY: Have the children imitate the movement of a bouncing acorn, a floating poplar seed and a spinning maple seed. Now they are ready to play the Travel'n Seed game!

VOCABULARY: imitate

LEAF AND SEED MOBILE (pp.13-14)

DISCUSSION: In collecting leaves, have the children noticed that maple leaves can vary in size and color? Is this also true of poplar and oak leaves? Does the basic shape remain the same, so the tree type can still be easily identified? Will a poplar ever look like an oak or maple leaf?

LEARNING ACTIVITY: Mount collected leaves of oak, maple and poplar individually on cards. Cover with clear Con-Tact. Have children sort by type and then by size and color.

EXTENDING ACTIVITY: If pairs of similar leaves of the same type can be found, the cards can be used for a Concentration card game by scrambling pairs and placing face down on table. (Can be played by 2 to 4 players at a time, with at least 10 to 15 pairs of leaf cards.) Players take turns placing two cards face up. If they match, they have earned a pair, but must also identify the type of leaf. If they do not match, cards are turned face down in same location and play continues counter-clockwise. The player with the most pairs wins.

VOCABULARY: size, similar, different, sort

BUILD-A-TREE   (pp.15-16)

DISCUSSION: With what parts of an oak tree are the children familiar? Discuss **roots**--"food lines" in the ground; **bark**--protection for the trunk; **trunk**--the body of a tree and support for the branches; **branches**--the growing place for **leaves, flowers** (catkins), **seeds** (acorns).

LEARNING ACTIVITY: Children complete pages 15 and 16, by cutting out pictures of oak tree parts and gluing in appropriate squares around tree.

Answer Key:

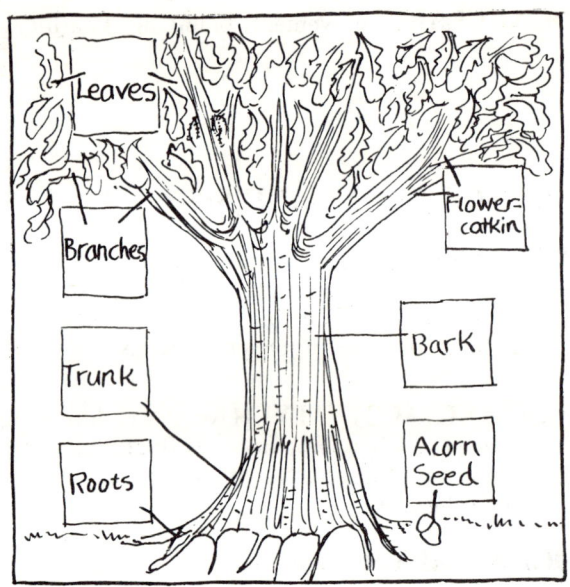

VOCABULARY: roots, trunk, bark, branches, protection, support, catkin flower

ANIMAL AIDS   (pp.17-18)

DISCUSSION: Plants would have a difficult time without the assistance of animals and, of course, animals need plants, too. Why do animals need plants? (food) Insects, like bees and butterflies, feed on sweet nectar in the center of flowers. How else does a bee use nectar? (to make honey) While feeding on the flower nectar, hairs on the insect's legs and body catch pollen powder. As other flowers are visited by the insect, what happens to this powder? If it drops off, the other flowers will be able to make seeds.

Many birds like to eat berries that grow on some plants. The berries contain seeds and are dropped on the ground by the birds as they eat. How does this help the plants?

What animal have we met earlier in this book that likes to bury nuts to eat in the winter?

LEARNING ACTIVITY: The "Root Clues" to the seed inside the acorn nut can be discovered by your "Tree Detectives" with another easily accomplished experiment. On an outing, point out protruding roots around the base of older trees and collect some acorns. (Avoid acorns with visible holes unless you wish to discover a hard-headed weevil larvae, as acorn weevils lay eggs inside some nuts in late summer.) Place several acorns on moist paper towels in a covered plastic container and set the container in a dark, warm area. The children should notice white roots growing from the acorn seeds in about one week -- a sure sign there is a tiny plant inside. Explain that roots help feed plants and recall any surface tree roots noticed on your outing.

Answer Key: Children draw squares around **4** butterflies and **10** bees pictured. They should circle **3** birds on the berry bush. There are **4** squirrels to color brown.

VOCABULARY: insects, nectar, pollen powder, birds, scatter

FURRY FARMERS AND HITCHHIKER SEEDS   (pp.19-20)

DISCUSSION: Can the children name some furry animals? Can they think of any animals with rather smooth skin? Some seeds easily stick to animal fur. What might an animal do if it finds seeds stuck in its furry coat? How do furry animals help plants?

LEARNING ACTIVITY: Conduct the experiment described on page 20. Discuss the children's conclusions.

Surface plant some "hitchhiker" seeds in potting soil. Keep in warm location and moisten with water using a spray or misting bottle. After several days look for signs of new plant life.

Answer Key: Color the following furry animals -- raccoon, mouse, two bunnies, deer, chipmunk
Do not color -- snake, toad, turtle

VOCABULARY: furry, smooth, hitchhiker, catch, burr

SCIENCE SING-A-LONG   (pp.21-22)

DISCUSSION: Can the children name some nonliving things? (rocks, toys, paper, bubble gum) How do we know these are nonliving? (They cannot change unless something living changes them. For example, children can make some toys work; paint white paper red; chew gum and blow a bubble, etc.)

What makes living things different from nonliving? (Living things can grow and change.) Name some living things. (Don't forget plants!)

Many living things, while they are growing, must change form completely or look different in order to continue living. For butterflies to live (or exist) they must be eggs and crawling caterpillars before they are ready to change into butterflies. The helpful honey bees change completely from eggs to grown-up bees right inside their beehive. Toads begin as eggs and pollywogs in a pond. Soon the pollywogs grow legs and finally hop out of the water as tiny toads, ready to live on the land so they can finish growing into large adult toads.

Metamorphosis (Met-a-'mor-fa-sis) is a word that says living things change form completely. It is such a special word, we can even sing a song about it.

30